OPEN THE DOORS OF YOUR LIFE
—*WORDS OF LIGHT* IN JAPANESE AND ENGLISH—
vol. 4

EDITED BY SEICHO TANIGUCHI
TRANSLATED BY DEAN TAKAO MAKINODAN
REVISED BY CHRISTOPHER NORTON-WELSH

Published by Nippon Kyobunsha Co. Ltd.,
6-44, Akasaka 9-chome, Minato-ku, Tokyo 107-8674.
No part of this publication may be reproduced
in any form or by any means without permission
in writing from the publisher.
Copyright © 2008 by Seicho Taniguchi.
All rights reserved. Printed in Japan.

First Edition 2008

ISBN978-4-531-05262-2

人生の扉を開く ④

日英対訳で読む
ひかりの言葉

OPEN THE DOORS OF YOUR LIFE
WORDS OF LIGHT IN JAPANESE AND ENGLISH vol.4

谷口清超監修
EDITED BY SEICHO TANIGUCHI

英訳　牧之段高男ディーン
監訳　クリストファー・ノートンウェルシュ

日本教文社

はじめに

　本書は、生長の家総裁・谷口清超先生が監修されている日めくりカレンダー『ひかりの言葉』の日英対訳版です。これまでに第1集（2005年刊）、第2集（2006年刊）、第3集（2007年刊）と3冊刊行され、不透明な時代を生きる人々に光をもたらすメッセージ集として好評をいただいております。

　今回はその第4集、1996年〜1998年の3カ年分を一冊にまとめました。端的に指針が示された主文と、それを詳しく説明した脇文とからなる、毎年精選された31日分の真理の言葉は、読む人に勇気と明るい希望を運んでくれます。

　私たちはいま、環境問題やグローバル化した経済問題など、地球規模でものごとを考えなければならない時代に遭遇し、個人の欲望を超えた広い視野に立った生き方が求められています。この「人生の扉を開く」シリーズは、そんな時代にこそ、ますます光を放ちます。

　本書が、これまでの生活を振りかえり、地球規模の広い視野に立った生活に転換するための道しるべとなり、幸福な人生の扉を開く心の糧となることを願っております。

日本教文社

Preface

This book is a Japanese-English edition of the calendar, *Words of Light*, which is edited by Rev. Seicho Taniguchi, President of Seicho-No-Ie. So far three volumes have been published: the first in 2005, the second in 2006 and the third in 2007. These have been well received as enlightening messages for our turbid age.

This fourth volume has brought together calendar selections from 1996 to 1998. The straightforward guiding words of the main text are followed by a detailed explanation. The words of Truth of the thirty-one carefully selected writings for each year bring courage and bright hope to their readers.

We are in age that requires thinking on a global scale, whether it be about environmental problems or about the globalized economy. What is needed is a way of life that goes beyond personal desires. The *Open the Door of Your Life* series is indeed bringing even more light to our age.

We hope that this book will become a guide to reflecting on our daily lives and to changing ourselves to live lives that are grounded in broadmindedness on a global scale, and will also serve as the mental sustenance for opening the doors to a happy life.

Nippon Kyobunsha

目 次
CONTENTS

1996 ·················· 7

1997 ·················· 71

1998 ·················· 135

参考図書　References······198

1996

★
ひかりの言葉
WORDS OF LIGHT

1
人間は宇宙の大生命と一つにつながっている

　われは神と一体である。神は宇宙に満ちていたまう。宇宙に満つる力と自分は一体なのである。その大いなる力が底打つ濤のように自分の生命の内には動いているのである。その大いなる力は無限の智慧であり、わが計画する事物を導いて必ず最高の結果にまで成就して下さるのである。

（谷口雅春著『聖経版　真理の吟唱』より）

Man is joined in oneness with the Great Life of the universe.

We are one with God. God fills the universe. I am one with the power that fills the universe. That mighty power is moving within my life like a deep sea current. That mighty power is infinite wisdom. It guides my plans and realizes the greatest possible results.

From *Seikyôban Shinri no Ginshô* (Meditations on Truth, sutra edition) by Masaharu Taniguchi.

2

心をひらけば、
何時(いつ)でも何処(どこ)にでも機会(チャンス)がある

　神様はすでに私達に数々の善(よ)きものを与えておられるのであります。しかし、どんなに沢山(たくさん)善いものが与えられていても、それを見る「心の眼(め)」が開けていなければ、それは宝の持ちぐされです。神様から与えられている恩恵を、心から感謝し讃嘆(さんたん)するようになることが大切であります。

（谷口清超ヒューマン・ブックス2『運命の主人公』より）

Open your mind's eye and opportunities are present everywhere.

God already provides us with many good things. Nevertheless, no matter how many good things we are given, if our *mind's eye* to see them is not open, they are useless possessions. It is important to be sincerely grateful for and praise the blessings from God.

From *Unmei no Shujinkô* (Master of Destiny), Taniguchi Seicho Human Books, vol. 2.

3
花びらが降るように
良き言葉を雨降らせよ

　善き言葉は空から花びらが降るような、音楽が聞えてくるような美しい感じがします。皆さんの口から常に花びらのような良い言葉が出るようになったら、そこがこの世の極楽となり天国となるのであります。先ず家族同士仲よくして互いに褒め合う事です。褒める言葉ぐらい結構な事はないのであります。

（谷口雅春著『人生読本』より）

Let us use good words like a shower of beautiful flower petals.

Like flower petals from heaven and music, there is something beautiful about good words. If good words like flower petals always come from our mouth, an earthly paradise and heaven appear before us. Family members should first be on good terms and praise one another. There is nothing finer than words of praise.

From *Jinsei Dokuhon* (Life's Reader) by Masaharu Taniguchi.

4
真に「生きる」とは「今を生きる」ことである

　いかに努力している時でも、眉間(みけん)に八の字の皺(しわ)をよせて、歯ぎしりして頑張(がんば)っていたのでは、本当の力が出て来ない。つねに明るい希望をもって、力一杯全力投球をするのだ。少々の失敗で、へこたれてはならぬ。常に今を生き抜くと、一瞬一瞬が生きて輝いてくるのだ。何たる素晴らしき人生であることよ。

（谷口清超著『輝く日々のために』より）

To *live* genuinely is to *live the present moment to the fullest*.

No matter how hard we work, our true strength does not appear when are knitting our brow and grinding our teeth. While always keeping bright hope in our heart, we do our very best with all our strength. We must not be discouraged because of a small failure. When we always live the present to the fullest, every moment is alive and shining. How wonderful is human life!

From *Kagayaku Hibi no Tame ni* (For a Shining Daily Life) by Seicho Taniguchi.

5
あなたの欲するものは、既にあなたの内にある

　あなたが真に必要として求めるものは、既に"霊の世界"に於てはあなたの掌中にあるのである。既にあなたの掌中にあればこそ、そのあ̇る̇ことを直感してそれを実現したくなるのである。だからイエスは「求むるに先立ちて神はなくてならぬものを知り給う」といっていられるのである。

（谷口雅春著『新版　栄える生活365章』より）

What you seek is already in your hands.

Whatever you seek and you truly need are already in your hands in the "world of Spirit." Because it is already within your hands you know intuitively of its *existence* and want to realize it. That is why Jesus taught: "Your Father knoweth what things ye have need of, before ye ask him."

From *Shinpan Sakaeru Seikatsu 365 Shô* (365 Keys to a Prosperous Life, new edition) by Masaharu Taniguchi.

6

結果を求めない愛は、常によき果実を結ぶ

　太陽は、ただ照っている。そして何らの報酬も求めない。小川は、ただ流れている。水はうるおし、地下水となってわき出る。海は、ただ船をうかべ、魚を養い、汚物を静かに呑み込んで、平静であり、常に清浄である。それが「神の愛」である。神の愛こそ、真の人間の愛である。

（谷口清超ヒューマン・ブックス6『人生の開拓者』より）

The love that seeks no reward always brings good results.

The sun simply shines and it seeks nothing in return. A stream merely flows. Water gives moisture to the earth, goes underground and bubbles up to the surface. The sea only keeps ships afloat, sustains sea life, quietly swallows filth, is peaceful and always pure. This is the *Love of God*. The Love of God is indeed the love of the true human being.

From *Jinsei no Kaitakusha* (Pioneers of Human Life), Taniguchi Seicho Human Books, vol. 6.

7

「感謝」する心の中にこそ「天国」がある

　感謝の心は人生に希望を与える。人生の希望は人間に「生きる力」を与える。それは人間の肉体を健康にし、環境を美しくととのえる気力を与えるのである。「感謝の心」の中にこそ、神があらわれ、凡(すべ)てをいやし給うのである。感謝の心以外に、よい世界をつくる原動力はどこにもないのである。

　　　　　　　（谷口清超著『智慧と愛のメッセージ』より）

Heaven is indeed found in a *grateful* mind.

A mind of gratitude gives hope to life. Hope in life gives human beings the *power to live*. It is the energy for a healthy body and a beautiful environment. It is truly within the *mind of gratitude* that God appears and all things are healed. Except in the mind gratitude, the motive power for a good world is no where to be found.

From *Chie to Ai no Message* (Messages of Wisdom and Love) by Seicho Taniguchi.

8

当り前のことができる者は
賢人である

　天地の大道は何もむつかしいことはない、平々凡々のところに天地の道があるのである。道は病気になるものではないから、吾々の生活が平々凡々何の変哲もないところに無限無尽の有難さが感じられるようになれば、その生活は道に乗ったのであるから、病気は自ら癒えるのである。

（新選谷口雅春法話集 5『光明道中記』より）

Those who can do the ordinary are wise.

There is nothing difficult about the great path of the universe. This great path is within the commonplace and ordinary. Since the way never falls ill, our life rides on the way and illness heals of itself when we feel infinite and boundless gratitude for the commonplace, the ordinary and the everyday happenings.

From *Kômyô Dôchûki* (Record of the Journey of Light), Shinsen Taniguchi Masaharu Hôwashû, vol. 5.

9

使えば使うほど、
殖えてくるのが生命力である

　心の力、肉体の力、そのほかどんな力でも之を強め、増し、大きくする秘訣があります。それは難かしいことではありません。それは今ある力を十分使うことです。人間は、心の力でも、肉体の力でも、仕事をする力でも、勉強する力でも、使えば使うほど強くなり、増してくるのです。（谷口雅春著『人生読本』より）

What increases with use is the power of life.

There is a secret for strengthening, increasing and magnifying the power of the mind, the body and any other power. It is not difficult to do so. The secret is to fully use the power that we have at the present moment. The power of the mind, the power of the body, the power for work and the power for study become stronger with use and increase.

From *Jinsei Dokuhon* (Life's Reader) by Masaharu Taniguchi.

10
すべての人を赦すとき、心は必ず朗かになる

　人を赦すということは、実にすばらしい。過去にどんなことがあっても、それに引っかかり、相手を恨んだり憎んだりしていると、絶対に幸福にはなれない。一切のものを赦し、愛し、感謝する心になると、最高の幸せを得る。人を赦した時、損をするものは、誰一人いないのである。（谷口清超著『純粋に生きよう』より）

Our minds are sure to brighten when we forgive everybody.

To forgive someone is truly wonderful. No matter what may have happened in the past, we can never be happy if we are caught up with it, hold a grudge or hate another. When we forgive all people and things, love them and are grateful to them, we gain the greatest happiness. No one has ever suffered a loss through forgiveness.

From *Junsui ni Ikiyô* (Let Us Live a Pure Life) by Seicho Taniguchi.

11
執着を放ち神に全托せよ、必ずすばらしい結果となる

　神にまかせて解決しない問題は存在しない。人間にとって実に複雑きわまる問題のように見えても、神から見れば少しも複雑な問題ではない。我の力で解決しようと云う自力的態度を捨て、神の無限の叡智に信じてまかせてしまったならば、神は必ずや、調和と秩序を回復して下さるに相違ないのである。

（谷口雅春著『新版　真理』第9巻より）

Release your attachments and trust in God! Wonderful results will be yours.

There is never a problem that is not solved when we trust in God. A problem that is most complicated for a human being is by no means so for God. Discard your self-power thinking of solving things through your own strength, and believe and trust in God's infinite wisdom. When we do so God will certainly restore harmony and order.

From *Shinpan Shinri* (Truth, new edition), vol. 9 by Masaharu Taniguchi.

12
常に微笑(びしょう)せよ、少なくとも今日一日は必ず微笑せよ

　微笑(びしょう)は神様のつくりたまえる完全な世界を現像(げんぞう)するに必要な光です。明るい微笑は、魂にさしのぼる太陽の光みたいなものです。口の縁(ふち)を上に引き上げ、眉(まゆ)の間をひろげ、眼尻(めじり)をさげて愉快(ゆかい)に微笑して御覧(ごらん)なさい。心の不景気はふっ飛んでしまいます。愉快に、楽しく、明るく、笑いましょう。

　　　　　　　　（谷口雅春著『新版　真理』第 1 巻より）

☀☀☀☀☀

Always smile!
At least for today be sure to smile!

A smile is the light that is essential to bring the perfect world of God into the phenomenal world. A bright smile is like sunlight for the soul. Bring up the corners of your mouth, remove the furrow from your brow, cease to glare at others and wear a pleasant smile. Your mental gloom will be cast away. Let us smile pleasantly, happily and cheerfully.

From *Shinpan Shinri* (Truth, new edition), vol. 1 by Masaharu Taniguchi.

13

あなたには無限力があり無限生命がある

　われわれは、人間を「肉体」とみないのであって、「神の子」であると観るのである。人間は、肉体ではなく、永生の霊であり、その中に既に「無限」を抱いている存在である。その「無限」はわれわれが開発しなければあらわれないが、開発しさえすればいくらでも顕現するところの力である。

　（谷口清超ヒューマン・ブックス9『善意の世界』より）

Within you there is infinite power and infinite life.

We do not see human beings as *physical bodies* but as *children of God*. A human being is not a physical body but an immortal spirit that already possesses the *infinite* within. That *infinite* will not appear unless we develop it. Nevertheless, it is power that appears to its full extent by just developing it.

From *Zen-i no Sekai* (World of Good Intentions), Taniguchi Seicho Human Books, vol. 9.

14

愛を与え、知恵を与えて、「神の子」を生きよ

　神様の御心は、「与えて、与えて、与えつくせよ」と教えておられるのであります。それでもなお、ありあまるほどの幸福が与え返されるのが、「神様の世界の夫婦生活」であり、家庭生活であります。「与えたら減る」のは物の世界でありますが、神様の世界は「与えたら必ずふえる」のであります。

（谷口清超新書文集5『「愛」は勝利する』より）

Give love, give wisdom and live as a *child of God*!

God's Mind teaches: "Give, give, give of yourselves completely!" Be that as it may, the state of a superabundance of happiness returning to us is the *married life of God's world* and family life. That *things decrease by giving* is a fact of the world of matter, but the world of God is that *things surely increase when we give.*

From *"Ai" wa Shôrisuru* (Love Wins), Taniguchi Seicho Shinshobunshû, vol. 5.

15

生活が「道」に乗るとき、病苦は自ら癒えるのである

　人間が幸福になるためには、幸福になる道に乗らなければならない。「幸福になる道」とは、そのまま当り前に人間の本性に順い、人間の本性に生きて行く道であります。父母に感謝し、夫婦互いに感謝し、子に感謝するのは人間の本性でありまして、それを実行するのは何も難かしいことはないのです。

　　　　　（谷口雅春著作集第9巻『幸福の哲学』より）

When our life rides on the *way*, the suffering from illness heals of itself.

For human beings to be happy, they must ride on the *way of happiness*. The way of happiness is to follow the original nature of a human being as it is, and in an ordinary manner, and live that original nature. To be grateful to our parents, to our spouse and our children is the original nature of a human being. It is not at all difficult to do this.

From *Kôfuku no Tetsugaku* (Philosophy of Happiness), Taniguchi Masaharu Chosakushû, vol. 9.

16

隠れたるところにて、人を賞め得る人となれ

　人の心は皆一つに連なっているから、ひとの善いことやすばらしさを、その人ではない人に話をしても、いつかはその人の耳にも届くものだ。目の前で相手の美点をほめるより、この方がずっとおくゆかしいとも言える。そしてどのくらい相手を高めあげ、お互いに心から打ちとけ合えるか知れないのである。

　　　　　　　（谷口清超著『智慧と愛のメッセージ』より）

Become a person who can praise others when unseen.

Since our minds are joined in oneness, when we speak about another's good points and wonderful abilities to someone, other than the person himself, those words will reach him someday. This is far more refined than to praise a person in his presence. There is no way of knowing how greatly this enhances the self-worth of another and builds mutual understanding with him.

From *Chie to Ai no Message* (Messages of Wisdom and Love) by Seicho Taniguchi.

17
人生の雨は、晴れ上(あが)った日を迎える"浄化作用"である

　雨上(あが)りの朝の日射(ひざ)しほどすがすがしいものはない。雨の夜は、陰鬱(いんうつ)であるが、その中に、宇宙を浄化する静かな働きが秘(ひ)められている。人生の雨も、結局はカラリと晴れ上った朝のために現れる"浄化作用"に他(ほか)ならない。失敗や困難をおそれるな。必ず「明るいすがすがしい朝」が訪れることを信ぜよ。

（谷口清超著『伸びゆく日々の言葉』より）

The rain that falls in human life is the "purification" to welcome sunny days.

There is nothing more refreshing than the morning sun after the rain. While the night rain is dreary, hidden within it is the quiet work that purifies the universe. The rain in human life is ultimately nothing but the "purification" for the clear, bright morning. Do not fear failures and difficulties. Believe that the *clear and refreshing morning* is sure to come.

From *Nobiyuku Hibi no Kotoba* (Daily Words for Growth) by Seicho Taniguchi.

18

あなたがあなたを好きになれば、
全ての人があなたを好きになる

　あなたが人から愛され、尊敬されることを望むなら、先ずあなたがあなた自身を愛し尊敬することだ。あなたがあなたを軽蔑すれば、全ての人はその如くあなたを軽んずる。あなたがあなたを好きになれば、皆がそのように同調する。何故なら、あなたの人生を支配する者は、あなた自身だからである。

　　　　　　　（谷口清超著『伸びゆく日々の言葉』より）

When you learn to love yourself, you will be loved by all.

If you seek to be loved and respected by others, you must first love and respect yourself. If you look down on yourself, all people will do the same to you. If you come to like yourself, everyone will treat you in the same way. That is because it is you who rules your own life.

From *Nobiyuku Hibi no Kotoba* (Daily Words for Growth) by Seicho Taniguchi.

19
この世の中に、無駄なものは一つもない

　世の中に無駄なものは一つもない。困難さえもその人に知能を賦与する。困難の中にあって毅然として立つ者には荘厳の美が備わる。困難は吾々に或る価値を賦与する。困難は困難にあらず、平易は平易にあらず、曲るべきは曲り、屈すべきは屈し、或は峻しく或は急にして生命愈々美しく荘厳を極む。

　　　　　（谷口雅春著『新版　光明法語〈道の巻〉』より）

Not a single experience in life is wasted.

Not a single experience in life is wasted. Even difficulties are the bearers of intelligence. Those who stand firm in the face of difficulty are provided with a solemn beauty. Difficulty is the bearer of value. Difficulty is not difficulty, the easy is not easy, what must bend will bend, what submits will submit and so, perhaps sternly or unexpectedly, does life increasingly achieve a solemn beauty.

From *Shinpan Kômyôhôgo: Michi no Maki* (Sermons on Light: Volume on the Way, new edition) by Masaharu Taniguchi.

20

「逃げ出そう」とすると、却って同じ環境が追いかけて来る

　何事によらず、人生からは「逃げ出す」ことはよくないのです。「逃げ出そう」とすると、かえって同じような境遇が追いかけて来るものです。何故なら「環境は心の影」であり、自分の心にふさわしい問題だけが自分の周囲にあらわれて来るという原則になっているからです。　　　　（谷口清超著『妻として母として』より）

If we *run away*, the same circumstances will only follow us.

Not matter what it may be, to *run away* from things in life is never desirable. If we *run away*, the same circumstances will only follow us. That is because the *environment is a shadow of the mind* and there is the basic principle that only problems appropriate to our state of mind appear in our surroundings.

From *Tsuma Toshite Haha Toshite* (As a Wife and Mother) by Seicho Taniguchi.

21
自分の殻(から)を捨て切ったとき、永遠(いのち)の生命を自覚する

　多くの病者はこれから健康になろうとして、健康法を励行(れいこう)するが、思うように効果が挙(あ)がらないのは、これからと思っているからである。既(すで)に今、健康であるのである。肉体は自分ではない。自分の殻(から)である。殻何するものぞ。捨(す)て切れ、捨て切れ、捨て切ったとき永遠の生命(いのち)と、今茲(ここ)にある天国を知る。

　　　　　　（新選谷口雅春法話集 5『光明道中記』より）

✺ ✺ ✺ ✺ ✺

When we completely discard our shell, we awaken to eternal life.

A good number of sick people do not achieve the results they desire despite their strict observance of hygiene with the belief of becoming healthy *in the future*. This is because their thoughts are focused *on the future*. At the *present moment*, we are already healthy. The physical body is not ourself. It is our shell. What good is a shell? Discard it completely! Throw it away! When we have done so, we will know eternal life and heaven that is here and now.

From *Kômyô Dôchûki* (Record of the Journey of Light), Shinsen Taniguchi Masaharu Hôwashû, vol.5.

22

人が明るく努力するとき、
成功への路(みち)を確実に進む

　生命(せいめい)は光の中で育ち、闇(やみ)の中では育たない。何故(なぜ)なら太陽の光のエネルギーをうけて生命は現象化するからだ。物質や動植物(どうしょくぶつ)ばかりではなく、人の心も光を失うと生長を損(そこな)う。常に明るくあれ。明るい心で学習すると、どんどん進歩する。その進歩がまた心の明るさを呼びさまし、進歩の引金(ひきがね)を引くのである。

　　　　　　（谷口清超著『伸びゆく日々の言葉』より）

When we do our best with happiness in our heart, we surely advance on the path to success.

Life grows in light and not in darkness. That is because life takes form in the phenomenal world by receiving the energy from sunlight. This is true for not only matter, plants and animals, but the human mind also fails to grow when light is lost. Always be happy! When we study with a happy mind, we make rapid progress. That progress again summons happiness and initiates new progress.

From *Nobiyuku Hibi no Kotoba* (Daily Words for Growth) by Seicho Taniguchi.

23
心に想_{おも}うことは、
人生に種_まくことである

　わたしたちは、美しき、愛深き、愉_{たの}しき、明るき、光に満_みちた、健_{すこ}やかな、生き生きとした積極的な想念を宇宙の創造の沃地_{よくち}に播_まかなければならないのである。そのような想念を常に起こしているならば、それが種子_{たね}となって発芽し、ついに現象界に生長して、現実によき果_みを結ぶことになるのである。

　　　　　　　（谷口雅春著『如意自在の生活365章』より）

To think is to sow seeds in human life.

We must sow beautiful, deeply loving, pleasant, happy, light-filled, healthy, energetic and positive ideas in the universe's fertile land of creation. By always sowing these ideas, they become seeds that sprout and ultimately grow in the phenomenal world and finally produce good fruit.

From *Nyoi Jizai no Seikatsu 365 Shô* (365 Golden Keys to a Completely Free Life) by Masaharu Taniguchi.

24
仕事に高下(こうげ)はない、何を如何(いか)なる態度でするかが問題だ

　或(あ)る風呂番(ふろじ)の爺(じい)さんは、実に丁寧(ていねい)に深切(しんせつ)に全(すべ)ての人の背中を流してやっていた。仕事の貴(とうと)さは全く体裁(ていさい)やみえによるのではないのです。どれだけ真心(まごころ)をこめて人々の幸福と安寧(あんねい)と発展のために奉仕するかというその人の心の中に貴い何ものにもかえがたい宝がかくされているのであります。

（谷口清超ヒューマン・ブックス１『愛と祈りを実現するには』より）

There is no high or low to work. What we do and our attitude to it is important.

An elderly bath attendant at a public bath washes the back of each user most kindly and with great care. The value of our work is completely unrelated to *appearance* and style. Hidden within the mind of a person, who works devotedly with sincerity in his heart for the happiness, peace and prosperity of others, is a precious and irreplaceable gem.

From *Ai to Inori o Jitsugensuru ni wa* (To Realize Love and Prayer), Taniguchi Seicho Human Books, vol. 1.

25
目立たない仕事の報いは天の倉に貯えられる

　人から見て目覚ましい仕事を為すということは、それはすでに報いを受けたのであるから、それほどの価値はないのである。すべての人生の出来事と環境において、人から見て目立たない仕事を人のために尽くすとき、その報いは天の倉に貯えられるのである。すべての善は神よりのみ来るのである。

（谷口雅春著『生命の實相』頭注版第38巻より）

The reward from work that goes unseen is stored in the vault of heaven.

Work that is spectacular and conspicuous is not very valuable because it has already been rewarded. For all happenings and circumstances in life, when we labor devotedly for the sake of others at work that goes unseen, our reward is stored in the vault of heaven. All goodness comes from God alone.

From *Seimei no Jissô* (Truth of Life), vol. 38 by Masaharu Taniguchi.

26

"打出(うちで)の小槌(こづち)" とは あなたの笑顔と讃嘆(さんたん)である

　ニコニコしても、月給がふえるわけではなし、つまらんと思っている人は、まことに気の毒な人達である。すぐはふえなくても、やがて必ずふえてくる。月給どころか、一切の運命がよくなって、何もかも、いいことばかりが降(ふ)って来るのであるから、実に素晴らしい。

（谷口清超著『智慧と愛のメッセージ』より）

The "mallet of fortune" is your smile and words of praise.

Those who think that smiles are meaningless because they do not increase our monthly salary, are pitiful indeed. While our salary may not increase immediately, it will certainly do so before long. Far more than just salary, our entire destiny will improve and every good thing will come our way. That is why smiles are truly wonderful.

From *Chie to Ai no Message* (Messages of Wisdom and Love) by Seicho Taniguchi.

27
一人の人に対してする深切(しんせつ)は すべての人の幸福につながる

　人間は決して一人一人がバラバラな存在ではないのであって、皆が一つ"神の生命(いのち)"につながっている「神の子」同士であります。ですから、一人の人に対する深切(しんせつ)が、ただそれだけのものにとどまるものではなく、自分自身はもちろんのこと、他のすべての人々の幸福につながるのであります。

（谷口清超新書文集6『サラリーマンの精神衛生』より）

A kind deed to another is related to the happiness of all people.

Human beings are never separate and unrelated existences. All are kindred *children of God* who are joined in the one "Life of God." That is why a kind deed to another does not remain at that alone but it is linked, without doubt, to our own happiness and the happiness of all people.

From *Sararî-man no Seishin Eisei* (A Salaried Man's Mental Hygiene), Taniguchi Seicho Shinshobunshû, vol. 6.

28
愛する者を放つ時、最高の幸せが返ってくる

　相手を縛る時、相手は決してありの儘の完全な姿を現すものではない。良人を、妻を、子供を、本当に愛するならば、良人を、妻を、子供を、完全に自由に放たねばならない。愛する者を放つ時、最愛のものは自分のふところに帰ってくる。真に解放されたとき人間は必ずよくなるのです。

（谷口雅春著『新版　叡智の断片』より）

When you release the one you love, the greatest happiness returns to you.

When you tie a person down, his originally perfect self will never appear. If you truly love your husband, wife or child, you must completely release your mental attachment. When we release those we love, the greatest reward returns to our heart. Human beings are sure to improve when they have been truly released.

From *Shinpan Eichi no Danpen* (Short Pieces of Wisdom, new edition) by Masaharu Taniguchi.

29

一番苦しいと思う時、あなたは目的達成の寸前にいる

　コロンブスを乗せた帆かけ船の船員が待てども待てども新大陸が見つからないで失望して、今や将にコロンブスを監禁して船を引返そうとしていた時、彼は一層新大陸の間近まで来ていたのではないか。兄弟よ、陰極は陽転するのだ。失敗のたび毎に貴方の希望が実現に近づいている事を知れ。

　　　　（谷口雅春著『生命の實相』頭注版第20巻より）

☀ ☀ ☀ ☀ ☀

What seems to be the most trying moment is the instant before the fulfillment of your goal.

The crew of Columbus' ship had lost hope after the new continent was nowhere to be found after days of sailing, and were about to imprison him and turn the ship around. At that moment they were the closest to the new continent, were they not? Friends, the negative changes to the positive. With every failure you encounter, know that your hopes are on the verge of being realized.

From *Seimei no Jissô* (Truth of Life), vol. 20 by Masaharu Taniguchi.

30
神の護りは完璧にして、神の導きは完全である

　神は常に、その全能なる力をわれらに授け給い、全智なる智慧によって私たちを導き給う。神の護りは完璧にして、神の導きは完全であるから、私たちは常に迷うことなく、神の"内からなる導き"に全托して、大安心のもとに行動することができるのである。神は常に最も良き道を知り給う。

　　　　　　　（谷口雅春著『聖経版　真理の吟唱』より）

God's protection is thorough and His guidance is perfect.

God always gives us His almighty strength and guides us with His infinite wisdom. God's protection is thorough and His guidance is perfect. That is why we never lose our way, we completely trust in His "guidance from within" and we can engage in our work with great peace of mind. God always knows the best possible path.

From *Seikyôban Shinri no Ginshô* (Meditation on Truth, sutra edition) by Masaharu Taniguchi.

31
素直に信じ、行ずる者が、最後の勝利者となる

　人間はただ「感謝」さえしておれば、全てがうまく行くように出来ている「神の子」なのです。それを忘れて、色んなことに文句を言ったり、理屈をこね回していると、幸福にも健康にもなるものではない。何故なら人生とは、理屈ではなく、ただ素直に「神のいのちを生きる」ことだからです。

　　　　（谷口清超新書文集3『もっと幸福になれる』より）

Those who are honest and obedient in their faith and practice will succeed in the end.

Human beings are *children of God* who have been created to experience all good things if they would only be *grateful*. When they forget this and complain about various things and argue, they fail to become both happy and healthy. That is because human life is not an argument but simply to *live the life of God* honestly and obediently.

From *Motto Kôfuku ni Nareru* (We Can Become Happier), Taniguchi Seicho Shinshobunshû, vol. 3.

1997

★
ひかりの言葉
WORDS OF LIGHT

1

わが希望は既に成就せり

　われわれが心を神のみに集注して、神と全的に一体となる事が出来るならば、神の中には一切の"なくてならぬもの"が既にあるのであるから、そして神は、われわれが何を必要とするかを既に知り給うのであるから、唯、神と一体となる事によってのみ、願う事物が悉く叶えられることになるのである。

（谷口雅春著『聖経版　続　真理の吟唱』より）

☀☀☀☀☀

My hopes are already realized.

If we focus our mind only on God and if our actions can be completely one with God, since *all that we really need* already exists within God and God already knows these things, by simply becoming one with God alone, our wishes will be totally realized.

From *Seikyôban Zoku Shinri no Ginshô* (Meditations on Truth II, sutra edition), by Masaharu Taniguchi.

2

あなたは運命の主人公である

　あなたの心に「輝き」があれば、あなたの運命は必ず向上する。この世はあなたが作る人生劇(じんせいドラマ)であるから、輝きのある心は、舞台に「花」を咲(さ)かせるのである。それ故(ゆえ)、あなたの人生を支配する心に「輝き」をあらわせ。それには「神の子・人間」であることを知り、それを味わい、体験し、表現することだ。

（谷口清超著『伸びゆく日々の言葉』より）

You are the master of your destiny.

If there is *brightness* in your heart, your destiny is sure to improve. Since this world is a drama created by ourselves, a bright and cheerful mind causes *flowers* to bloom on the stage. That is why you must bring *brightness* into your mind, the ruler of your life. To do so you should know, savor, experience and express the truth that *human beings are children of God.*

From *Nobiyuku Hibi no Kotoba* (Daily Words for Growth) by Seicho Taniguchi.

3

神と偕(とも)なる自分に不可能はなし

　わたしたちは毎朝夕、神想観(しんそうかん)を行(ぎょう)じて、心を神に振り向けてひたすらとなり、神より新しき生命(せいめい)を受け、愛を受け、智慧(ちえ)を受け、それに培(つちか)われ、養われ、護(まも)られ、導かれているのである。私たちは背後を神に護られて進むのである。だから、わが為(な)さんと欲することは必ず成就するのである。

　　　　　　　　（谷口雅春著『聖経版　真理の吟唱』より）

There is nothing impossible for those who are one with God.

We practice Shinsokan every morning and night, turn our mind *solely* to God, receive new life, love and wisdom from Him, and are being fostered, raised, protected and guided by Him. We advance with God protecting us from behind. That is why what I want to accomplish is certain to be realized.

From *Seikyôban Shinri no Ginshô* (Meditations on Truth, sutra edition) by Masaharu Taniguchi.

4

ただ善(よ)き事のみを数え上げよ

　この世には素晴らしいことが一杯ある。だが面白(おもしろ)くないこともあるし、嫌(いや)なこともある。そのどちらでも見られるが、良いことや有難(ありがた)いことを見ていた方がずっと幸福になる。健康にもなり、仕事も繁栄するのである。それはこの世には「心で認めるものが現(あら)われて来る」という原則があるからだ。

　　　　　　　　　（谷口清超著『自己完成のために』より）

Count only the good things in your life.

This world is full of wonderful things. Nevertheless, there are also uninteresting things and unpleasant things. While we can see both the wonderful and the uninteresting, we are always happy when we see the good things and the things to be grateful for, and we enjoy good health and our business prospers. That is because there is the fundamental rule in this world that what *our mind recognizes will appear.*

From *Jiko Kansei no Tame ni* (For Our Self-Perfection) by Seicho Taniguchi.

5

いたる所に神の導きがある

　必要でないものは何も吾々(われわれ)の周囲にあらわれては来ない。環境は我が心の影(かげ)であると言うが、我が心の影なるが故(ゆえ)に、我が心にとって最も必要な訓練が外界に与えられるのである。世の中に悪(あ)しき人は一人もおらず、悪意ある環境は一つもなく、すべて良心の囁(ささや)きは、即(すなわ)ち神の導きである。

（谷口清超ヒューマン・ブックス1『愛と祈りを実現するには』より）

God's guidance is present everywhere.

What is not important will never appear in our surroundings. While we say that the environment is a shadow of our mind, because it is a shadow of our mind, we are provided in the external world with what is most important for our mental training. There is not a single evil person or harmful environment in this world. All the whispers of conscience are the guidance of God.

From *Ai to Inori o Jitsugensuru ni wa* (To Realize Love and Prayer), Taniguchi Seicho Human Books, vol. 1.

6

祈りこそ希望の扉を開く鍵である

「心の中に強く描(えが)いたことは必ず実現する」のであって、「祈りがかなえられる」のは当然であると言わなければなりません。ことに、私達の心の中に描かれる思いが、「神様の思い」に一致する時、その祈りの実現は、どんな力をもってしても押し止(とど)めることはできないのです。

（谷口清超ヒューマン・ブックス2『運命の主人公』より）

Prayer is indeed the key that opens the doors of hope.

What we strongly envision is sure to be realized and we must say that it is only natural that *our prayers are realized.* This is particularly true of our thoughts that are in accord with the *thoughts of God.* The realization of such prayers cannot be stopped no matter what efforts are made to do so.

From *Unmei no Shujinkô* (Master of Destiny), Taniguchi Seicho Human Books, vol. 2.

7

愛のことばが最高の贈物だ

　愛のこもったやさしい言葉は、これを受けた人を幸福にすると共に、これを与えた人自身をも幸福にする。冷たい憎悪を含んだ言葉は、発する人自身が先ず不幸になり、それを投げられた人の心をくだく。愛のこもった深切な言葉は、相手に対して強壮剤として働くのである。愛語を惜しんではならない。

（谷口雅春著『新版　女性の幸福365章』より）

Words of love are the greatest gift.

Kind words that are filled with love bring happiness to their recipients and also those who convey them. Cold and hateful words first bring misfortune to those who send them and shatter the minds of their recipients. Kind words that are filled with love work on others like a tonic. You must not abstain from using loving words.

From *Shinpan Josei no Kôfuku 365 Shô* (365 Keys to Women's Happiness, new edition) by Masaharu Taniguchi.

8

深切の種子は、必ず善き果を結ぶ

　行動の結果がハッキリとあらわれてくるには、ある時間的ズレがある。ということは、善をしても、すぐその結果は出てこないということだ。しかしながら、原因の種子が播かれた以上、必ず結果が出るのである。このことを信じ、安心し、善行をなせ。愛行せよ。祖国と人類のために、まごころを捧げよう。

　　　　　（谷口清超著『輝く日々のために』より）

Seeds of kindness are sure to bear good fruit.

There is a time lag before the results of our actions appear clearly. In other words, the good that we do does not immediately bear fruit. Nevertheless, as long as the seeds of cause are sown, they are sure to produce results. Believe in this and engage in good and loving deeds with peace of mind. Work devotedly for the sake of the country and humankind.

From *Kagayaku Hibi no Tame ni* (For a Shining Daily Life) by Seicho Taniguchi.

9
必要なすべての物は おのずから整ってくる

　われは神の子である。されば、神の有ちたまえる全徳を身に実現する事ができるのである。神は無限の富の源泉であるから、必要なすべての物質はおのずと何らかの経路を通して自分のところへやってくるのである。神の無限の供給が通ってくるところの通路は愛であるから私はつねに愛を実践するのである。

（谷口雅春著『私はこうして祈る』より）

☀ ☀ ☀ ☀ ☀

All that I need will be provided of its own accord.

I am a child of God. That is why I can manifest within myself all the virtues of God. Since God is the source of infinite wealth, all the material things that I need will come to me of their own accord through some channel. The channel for God's infinite supply is love and for that reason I always practice love.

From *Watashi wa Kôshite Inoru* (This Is How I Pray) by Masaharu Taniguchi.

10
日々是好日、毎日いのちが新生する
にちにちこれこうじつ

　毎日毎日が勝利の日である。毎日毎日が健康の日である。日取の好し悪しを言ってはならない。すべての「日」は神の与えものである。神が、あなたの健康のために、神が、あなたの幸福のために、愛するために、歓ぶために、あなたにすべての「日」を与えたまうたのである。　　　　　（谷口雅春著『新版　真理』第9巻より）

Every day is a good day. Every day is a day for rebirth.

Every day is a day for success. Every day is a day for good health. It is not for you to say that the day is good or bad. All *days* are given to you by God. God has given you all *days* for your health, for your happiness, love and joy.

From *Shinpan Shinri* (Truth, new edition), vol. 9 by Masaharu Taniguchi.

11
和解と感謝の生活に、不幸は近よらない

　あなたの環境にも、あなたの心が現われる。あなたの心が乱れると、環境にも乱れが生じ、衝突する車に乗ったりする。それは決して偶然ではない。それ故日々心を整え、神の国に心を同調させ、和解と感謝の生活に入ることが大切である。すると自然法爾の生活が出来、流通自在の「大神通」が発揮できる。

（谷口清超著『伸びゆく日々の言葉』より）

Misfortune will never come near a life of reconciliation and gratitude.

Your mind also manifests itself in your environment. When you are agitated, trouble appears in your environment and you ride a car that is involved in a collision. That is by no means a coincidence. And that is why it is essential to order your mind daily, tune it to the Kingdom of God, and live a life of reconciliation and gratitude. In this way you can live a life of the spontaneous working of the universal law and demonstrate the *great supernatural power* of free circulation.

From *Nobiyuku Hibi no Kotoba* (Daily Words for Growth) by Seicho Taniguchi.

12

"感謝の念" は最良の治病薬だ

　心が落胆したり悩んだりすると、肉体の自衛力が減る。心の悩みがなくなり、穏やかな充ち足りた気持で感謝の生活を送るようになると、自然に生命力が出てきて、黴菌やビールスを体外に押し出す力が出る。つまり「自衛力」が回復する。これが「自然治癒」とか「免疫」とか言われるものである。

（谷口清超著『人は天窓から入る』より）

"Grateful thoughts" are the best medicine.

When we are discouraged or worried, our body's defenses weaken. When our troubles vanish and we live a life of gratitude with peaceful and happy thoughts, our life power naturally appears and we have the strength to expel germs and viruses from our body. That is to say, *our defenses* are restored. This is called *natural healing* or *immunity*.

From *Hito wa Tenmado Kara Hairu* (We Enter From Heaven's Window) by Seicho Taniguchi.

13
称讃(しょうさん)の言葉は、無限の「福」を引き出す

　人の美点を見て、それを称(ほ)め讃(たた)える事は非常に大切である。現象の奥に隠(かく)されている「実相」は、よき称讃のコトバによって、はじめて発掘されるのである。称讃すべき対象は、相手にある「美点」でなければならない。それは「実相」が現象にあらわれている箇所であるが故(ゆえ)に、「実相開顕(かいけん)」の起点となる。

　　　　　　（谷口清超著『人は天窓から入る』より）

☀︎☀︎☀︎☀︎☀︎

Words of praise draw out infinite *fortune*.

It is very important to see the good points of another and praise them. The *True Image*, which is hidden within phenomena, is extracted for the first time by good words of praise. The object of our praise must be another's *good points*. Since these are places where the *True Image* is being manifested in phenomena, they are a starting point for the *manifestation of the True Image*.

From *Hito wa Tenmado Kara Hairu* (We Enter From Heaven's Window.) by Seicho Taniguchi.

14

愛のあるところに、必ず神の導きがある

　よき思いつきは、常に「愛」と結合している。人々のお役に立ち、祖国のためになり、世界平和の確立に役立つ仕事をさせていただきたいという、燃ゆるような愛の思いがおこる時、その人には、素晴らしい智慧(ちえ)が天降(あまくだ)ってきて、そのフト思いつく考えが、非常に素晴らしい結果をもたらすのであります。

　　　　（谷口清超ヒューマン・ブックス4『生きる』より）

Where there is love, God's guidance is always present.

A good idea is always joined with *love*. When we are embraced by the love that is impassioned to work for the sake of others, the country or the establishment of world peace, wonderful wisdom descends from heaven and our sudden ideas bring extremely good results.

From *Ikiru* (To Live), Taniguchi Seicho Human Books, vol. 4.

15

生命（いのち）は生々（いきいき）と働くことによって生長する

　仕事や勉強は、人間が自分の生命（せいめい）（自分の内にある生きる力）を生かすために、神がくださったものであります。最も幸福な人間は、仕事をし、勉強をする喜びを知った人です。それは世の中に益（えき）を与え、人に益（えき）を与えながら、自分も益（えき）を与えられ、心に無限の歓（よろこ）びを味わいつつ、自分自身が進歩する道なのです。

（谷口雅春著『人生読本』より）

Our life grows through vigorous and steady work.

Work and study have been given to human beings by God to make the best use of their life (their indwelling power to live). The happiest people are those who know the joy of work and study. That is the way to make progress while benefiting the world and people, and ourselves, and savoring infinite happiness.

From *Jinsei Dokuhon* (Life's Reader) by Masaharu Taniguchi.

16

和(なご)やかな家庭には善(よ)き子が育つ

　赤ちゃんはお腹の中(なか)にいる時から学習しているし、父母の会話を聞いている。だから、夫婦がいつも仲よく、愛ふかく、明るい希望にみちた言葉で暮し、「きっといい子が生れるよ」とか、「うれしいね、たのしいね、有難(ありがた)いね」と話し合っていると、思っている通りのよい子が生れ、よい子に育つのである。

　　　　　　（谷口清超著『ステキな生き方がある』より）

Good children grow well in a peaceful and harmonious home.

A child learns from the time it is in its mother's womb and listens to its parents' conversation. That is why the child of their dreams will be born and grows up well when the parents' family life is always filled with harmonious, deeply loving words that are filled with bright hope and they intersperse their conversation: "A good child will surely be born"; "How happy, joyful and blessed are we."

From *Sutekina Ikikata ga Aru* (There Is a Fine Way to Live) by Seicho Taniguchi.

17

賞(ほ)める方向に、子供たちは伸びる

　人の生命(せいめい)の実相には無限の善徳や善(よ)き性質や善き行為が宿(やど)っている。それを引き出すのが称讃(しょうさん)の言葉の力である。子供を教育する場合には、特にその子供に欠(か)けていると思われる徳目(とくもく)が既(すで)に本当にあるかのように讃(ほ)める言葉を使うならば、その讃(ほ)められた方向に、その子供が本当に立派になって来るのである。

（谷口雅春著『新版　生活の智慧 365 章』より）

Children grow
in the direction of our praise.

Within a person's True Image of Life there lives infinite good virtue, good nature and good deeds. It is the power of words of praise that draws these out. When educating children, if our words of praise are particularly used in a way that seems to say that they really have the virtues they are lacking, they will actually become fine persons in the direction of our praise.

From *Shinpan Seikatsu no Chie 365 Shô* (365 Keys to Daily Wisdom, new edition) by Masaharu Taniguchi.

18
人間の身体(からだ)には、自然の癒(いや)す力が宿っている

　全(すべ)ての人が自然に治(なお)す力をもっている。人間はもともと立派に作られていて、病気なんかしないように出来ている。すばらしい生命力が、もうちゃんと備(そな)わっているのですから、それを「ありがたい」とみとめる心があれば、すぐにでも出て来て、病気も傷も、何でも癒(なお)してくれることになるのです。

（谷口清超著『病いが消える』より）

In the human body there is nature's healing power.

All people naturally possess healing power. Human beings were originally created as excellent beings who are never afflicted by illness or the like. Since they are perfectly provided with wonderful life power, it will immediately appear and heal illness, injury and everything else if we are *grateful* for this blessing.

From *Yamai ga Kieru* (Illness Vanishes) by Seicho Taniguchi.

19
晴れやかな笑いは、全ての人の栄養剤である

　笑いは、ただその人自身を、健康に愉快にするばかりではない。快活な人は、周囲に幸福と健康とをまいて歩く。明るい朗らかな深切な笑顔を向けられては、何人も幸福にならずにはいられない。そういう人が医者であれば、患者は医者の顔を見るだけでよくなったりするものである。

　　　　　（谷口雅春著『生命の實相』頭注版第7巻より）

Bright and cheerful laughter is the nutritional medicine of all people.

Laughter does not only bring good health and happiness to those who laugh. Cheerful and lively people sow happiness and good health wherever they go. No one cannot help but become happy in the presence of a bright, cheerful and kind smile. If the person with that smile is a doctor, his patients will improve by just looking at his face.

From *Seimei no Jissô* (Truth of Life), vol. 7 by Masaharu Taniguchi.

20

与えること多き者は、
刈(か)りとることの多き者だ

　われわれは広い心をもってまだまだ他(ひと)に多くを与えうることを知らねばならぬ。まだまだ多くの深切(しんせつ)を人に与えよ。まだまだ多くの賞讃(しょうさん)を人に与えよ。与えること多き者は、刈(か)りとること多き者だ。その刈り入れは天から来るのだ。与えること多ければ、天の与え給う賜(たまもの)の通路も大きいのだ。

（谷口雅春著『生命の實相』頭注版第7巻より）

The harvest is great for those who give of themselves greatly.

We must be broadminded and know that we can give so much more to others. Give far more kindness. Give more and more praise. Those who give of themselves greatly receive a great harvest. That harvest comes from heaven. When we give greatly the path for the gifts from heaven is also great.

From *Seimei no Jissô* (Truth of Life), vol. 7 by Masaharu Taniguchi.

21

よいコトバから素晴らしい人生が生まれる

　コトバは、すばらしい力をもっています。それは物理的な力ではありません。物理的な力を引きおこす"引き金"のような役を果たす「心の力」なのですから、よくよく注意して使うべきです。明るい、健康なコトバを使いましょう。そうすれば、必ず、健康や幸福が次々に訪れて来るようになるものです。

（谷口清超著『親と子の愛について』より）

From good words a wonderful life is born in this world.

Words have wonderful power. That power is not a physical force. Since words are a *mental power* that works like a "trigger" for physical force, they must be used with great care. Let us use bright, cheerful and healthy words. When we do so good health and happiness will surely visit us one after another.

From *Oya to Ko no Ai ni Tsuite* (About the Love of Parent and Child) by Seicho Taniguchi.

22

なろうと思うよりも、なれると思い努力せよ

「しよう」とか「成ろう」とかいう考えよりも、「できる」とか「成る」とかいう考えの方が力が強いのです。「心」で「成れる」と信じたときには、心のフィルムではすでにそう成っているのです。心のフィルムに描かれたことは、この世の中に本当に出てくるのです。人間は、なれると思うものになれるのです。

（谷口雅春著『人生読本』より）

Don't think "I want to," think "I can" and do your very best.

"I can" and "I will" are stronger thoughts than "I'll try" or "I want to." When the *mind* believes "I can," it is already that way on our mental film. What is portrayed on the mental film actually appears in this world. Human beings become what they believe they can be.

From *Jinsei Dokuhon* (Life's Reader) by Masaharu Taniguchi.

23

明るいコトバを使う人に、明るい運命が近づいてくる

　コトバこそ凡(すべ)てのもののつくり主(ぬし)である。朝起きて「ああ、気持がよい朝だ。今日もしっかりやろう」と、勢いよく寝床(ねどこ)をハネ起き、家族の一人一人に感謝のあいさつをする者には、断じて不幸も病気もよりついて来ない。その悦(よろこ)びの心が悦(よろこ)びの世界をつくり出し、喜ばしい出来事をまねき寄せるのである。

　　　　　　　（谷口清超著『智慧と愛のメッセージ』より）

A happy destiny approaches those who use happy words.

Words are indeed the creator of all things. "Oh, what a fine morning! I'll also do my best today!" Those who get up in the morning energetically and greet each member of their family with words of gratitude will never be approached by misfortune and illness. Their joyful mind creates a world of joy and invites happiness.

From *Chie to Ai no Message* (Messages of Wisdom and Love) by Seicho Taniguchi.

24

今が時なり、躊躇(ちゅうちょ)すべからず

　今から始めても、決して遅くはない。何も手をつけなかったら、いつまでたっても改善されない。「思い立ったが吉日(きちじつ)」と言うではないか。「これだ」と思いついたことは、スグ実行しよう。仕事の上だけではなく、家庭生活でも、心がまえの問題でも、「今を生きる」には、今すぐ実行することだ。

（谷口清超著『伸びゆく日々の言葉』より）

The time is now! You must not waver!

It is by no means too late to start now. Things will never improve if we never get to work. Isn't there the saying "The day the thought comes to us is a good day"? Let us immediately carry out the *good ideas* that come to mind. This is not only for work, but even for family life and questions on mental attitude, to *live the present moment* is to take action at once.

From *Nobiyuku Hibi no Kotoba* (Daily Words for Growth) by Seicho Taniguchi.

25

永遠に進歩する人となれ

　いかなる人間も、もうこの程度で結構だということはないのである。神は創造の神である。創造の神は同じ状態に停滞(ていたい)することを嫌い給(たま)うのである。常に新たなる一歩を加えよ。日々自己を改善し、自己の能力を改善し、自己の仕事を改善する人は、必ず他(た)の世の人々にぬきんでて輝かずにいられないのである。

　　　　　　　　　　（谷口雅春著『青年の書』より）

Become a person who makes eternal progress.

It is true of all people that we can never be satisfied by some degree of progress. God is the Creator. The Creator has a dislike for things that remain stagnant. Let us always add a new step. Those who daily improve themselves, their ability and their work, cannot help but surpass others and shine.

From *Seinen no Sho* (For Young People) by Masaharu Taniguchi.

26

富は横取りをせず、縦取りをすべし

　横取りと云うのは、有限の世界から物を取って来ることでありまして、それは必ず誰かと衝突するのであります。これには必ず奪い合いを生じ、戦いや争いが起ってまいります。縦取りというのは、神の世界から、無限の世界から、頂いて来ることであります。これは頂いても相手は減らない頂きようです。

　　　　（谷口雅春著『新版　幸福を招く365章』より）

Wealth should be received not horizontally but vertically.

Receiving wealth horizontally is to acquire things from the finite world. Our efforts to do so are certain to collide with others. This will surely lead to struggle, conflict and strife. To receive vertically is to receive from the World of God and the Infinite World. Wealth that is received vertically does not bring loss to others.

From *Shinpan Kôfuku o Maneku 365 Shô* (365 Keys That Summon Happiness, new edition) by Masaharu Taniguchi.

27

「今」を生きるとき、無限の力が湧き出でる

　あなたの内に宿っている力を「今」に集中したときにのみ、最大の能率を発揮することが出来る。あなたの内に宿っている力はあなたの想念の向うところに振向けられるのでありますから、今に生命を集中するとき「今」の一点は「久遠無限」に通ずるがゆえに無限の力が湧き出でて来ることになるのです。

　　　　　　　（谷口雅春著『新版　真理』第2巻より）

When you live the *present moment*, infinite power bubbles forth.

It is only when you focus the power that dwells within you on the *present moment* that you can achieve the greatest efficiency. Since the power within you is turned to where your thoughts are directed, infinite power bubbles forth when we focus our life on the present moment because this single point of the *present moment* is in touch with the *eternal infinite*.

From *Shinpan Shinri* (Truth, new edition), vol. 2 by Masaharu Taniguchi.

28

仕事に熱中せよ、
その道の達人となる

　人が何かに熟達(じゅくたつ)しようと思うならば、できるだけそれに熱中することである。「面白(おもしろ)い」と思って一心にやったことは、急速に上達する。年齢がどうのこうのということはない。遊びに夢中になって食事も忘れる子供がいるように、あなたも仕事に熱中すれば、必ずその道の達人になれる。

　　　　　　　（谷口清超著『伸びゆく日々の言葉』より）

Be immersed in your work! You will become an expert.

If you seek to master something, you should try to immerse yourself in it. There is rapid progress when you work wholeheartedly and with *interest*. Age is never a problem. In the same way that children forget about their meals when they are engrossed in play, if you immerse yourself in your work, you are sure to become an expert.

From *Nobiyuku Hibi no Kotoba* (Daily Words for Growth) by Seicho Taniguchi.

29

愛は最も強力な力である

　愛は最も強力なる力である。如何(いか)なる説き伏せも、如何(いか)なる議論も、如何(いか)なる懲罰(ちょうばつ)も相手を説伏(せっぷく)せしめることは出来ないが、愛のみ相手を説伏する事が出来るのである。議論すれば議論でやりかえされる。けれども愛すれば必ず相手に愛される。愛されて和(なご)やかにならないものは一人もないのである。

　　　　　（谷口雅春著『新版　光明法語〈道の巻〉』より）

Love is the greatest power.

Love is the greatest power. While arguments, verbal battles or punishments cannot persuade, love alone can do so. A verbal battle provokes the same. Nevertheless, we are sure to be loved in return when we love others. There is no one who does not become calm and friendly when loved.

From *Shinpan Kômyôhôgo: Michi no Maki* (Sermons on Light: Volume on the Way, new edition) by Masaharu Taniguchi.

30
心を美しく保(たも)て、いつまでも美しく生きられる

　肉体だけの美は夏の無花果(いちじく)の如(ごと)し。それは速(すみや)かに頽(たい)廃(はい)してくずれ去る。されど精神が肉体に反映する美は老人になるとも消え去らない。女性は容貌(ようぼう)の美だけに頼ってはならない。知性の輝きのある美こそ、本当に願うべき美であり、愛によって深められている美こそ女性に崇高の感じを与える。

（谷口雅春著『新版　女性の幸福365章』より）

Keep beauty in your heart and you will live beautifully forever.

A beautiful body alone is like a summer fig. It soon falls into decay and vanishes. However, the beauty, which is a reflection of the mind upon the body, does not disappear with age. Women must not rely on a beautiful countenance alone. The beauty that shines with intelligence, is indeed the beauty that we really seek, and it is beauty deepened through love that truly makes a woman sublime.

From *Shinpan Josei no Kôfuku 365 Shô* (365 Keys to Women's Happiness, new edition) by Masaharu Taniguchi.

31

我れは神の子、神の無限の富の後継者なり

　人間は神様の子でありますから、神のもち給う全ての御徳をそっくり受け継いでいるものであります。ですから、貧しく窮乏している筈はないのです。この宇宙の壮大を創造り給い、更に更に無限の次元の大宇宙の機構を創造り給うた神は、「豊かさ」を最大限度に有ち給うているのです。

（谷口清超ヒューマン・ブックス１『愛と祈りを実現するには』より）

I am a child of God—the heir to God's infinite wealth.

Since human beings are children of God, they completely inherit all the divine virtues in God's possession. That is why they could not possible be afflicted by want and poverty. God, the creator of the magnificence of the universe and the creator of the mechanism of the Great Universe of infinite dimension, is the possessor of the greatest degree of *abundance*.

From *Ai to Inori o Jitsugensuru ni wa* (To Realize Love and Prayer), Taniguchi Seicho Human Books, vol. 1.

1998

★
ひかりの言葉
WORDS OF LIGHT

1

神はあなたの内にあり。
呼べば応(こた)えて導き給(たま)う

　神は、実に、いま、あなたと偕(とも)にあるのである。神はいまあなたの内に偕(とも)にありて、常に呼べば応(こた)え、あなたを導いて、安全と幸福との世界に導きたまうのである。いま、あなたが立てるところに、坐(ざ)しているところに、あなたの周囲に、内に、到(いた)るところに神はいましたまうてあなたを護(まも)りたまう。

（谷口雅春著『新版　女性の幸福365章』より）

God exists within you. Call Him and He will answer you and guide you.

God is *really* one with you at this *moment*. God is *now* within you. If you always call Him, He will answer you, guide you and lead you to a world of safety and happiness. Where you are now standing, sitting, in your surroundings, within you and in all places, God is present and is protecting you.

From *Shinpan Josei no Kôfuku 365 Shô* (365 Keys to Women's Happiness, new edition) by Masaharu Taniguchi.

2

明るい心を持つ者は、無限の宝を持つ者である

　心を明るくし、いつも感謝にみちあふれた生活を送るようにすれば、肉体も健康になり、家庭も明るくなり、やがて町も、村もすばらしく気持のよい「地上天国」らしくなる。「心」を支配する事によって、何でも創造する事ができる。人間はすばらしい「神の愛(めぐ)し子」だという事を知らなくてはならない。

　　　　　　　（谷口清超著『創造的人生のために』より）

Those with a bright and cheerful mind are the possessors of infinite treasure.

If our mind is bright and cheerful and we lead lives that are brimming over with gratitude, our body enjoys good health, our family becomes happy, and, before long, the towns and villages also become wonderful and pleasant like an *Earthly Paradise*. By ruling our *mind* we can create anything. We must know that human beings are wonderful *dear children of God.*

From *Sôzôteki Jinsei no Tame ni* (For a Creative Life) by Seicho Taniguchi.

3

神の造られた世界に、不完全なものは何一つない

　神様のお創(つく)りになった世界は完全でありますから、病気、不幸、災難等(とう)はないのであります。本当の世界、これを実相と申しますが、それは絶対の健康、幸福の充(み)ち満(み)ちている世界であります。その世界は、吾々(われわれ)が「信じ」「観(み)る」ことによって現象世界に映(うつ)し出されて来るのであります。

（谷口清超ヒューマン・ブックス１『愛と祈りを実現するには』より）

✦✦✦✦✦

There is absolutely no imperfection in the world created by God.

Since the world that God created is perfect, there is no illness, misfortune, calamity or the like in that world. While we call that world the True Image, it is a world that is overflowing with absolute health and happiness. That world is reflected in the phenomenal world through our *belief* and *visualization*.

From *Ai to Inori o Jitsugensuru ni wa* (To Realize Love and Prayer), Taniguchi Seicho Human Books, vol. 1.

4

少しも求めずに愛せよ。
これが幸せになる秘訣である

　愛せよ、少しも求めずに愛せよ。これが愛の秘訣である。こんなに愛してやっているのに相手はこうだと批難するな。呟くな。愛は、その結果がどうなるからとて愛するのであってはならない。愛することそのことが神の道だから愛するのだ。愛することそのことが幸福だから愛するのだ。

　　　　　（谷口雅春著『生命の實相』頭注版第22巻より）

Love without seeking even the slightest in return! This is the secret to happiness.

Love! Love without seeking even the slightest in return! This is the secret of love. Do not criticize someone for not acknowledging your love! Do not grumble! We must not love because of the results that love can bring. We love because to love is the way of God. We love because to love is happiness.

From *Seimei no Jissô* (Truth of Life), vol. 22 by Masaharu Taniguchi.

5
夢を描け、未来はすでにあなたの中にある

　宇宙のありとあらゆるものはすべて想念によって現れてきたものである。吾々が心の中に夢を描き、吾々がこれから持ちたいと思うところのものの設計、輪郭、構図等を心に描くならば、それがやがて吾々を動かすところの具体的原動力となって、遂にはこの現象世界にその事物を実現するに到るのである。

（谷口雅春著『青年の書』より）

Dream! Already the future exists within you.

Everything in the universe has appeared through ideas. If we dream and envision a design, outline, plan and the like for what we seek, in due time it becomes a concrete motive power that finally realizes it in phenomenal world.

From *Seinen no Sho* (For Young People) by Masaharu Taniguchi.

6

持続的に想い念ずることが、あなたの人生となり、運命となる

　私たちが強く持続的に想い念ずることが、その人自身の人生となり、運命となるのである。あなたが今、何者であるかということは、何をあなたが持続的に想いつづけて来たかをあらわしている。暗い運命の人は、自分の想念を"暗いもの"から一転して"明るい方向"に向け換えなければならない。

　　　　　（谷口雅春著『新版　栄える生活365章』より）

What you constantly think about becomes your life and destiny.

What you strongly think constantly about becomes your life and destiny. What you are at the present moment is a reflection of what thoughts you have constantly held. Those with a dark destiny must change their thoughts completely from "darkness" to the "bright and cheerful."

From *Shinpan Sakaeru Seikatsu 365 Shô* (365 Keys to a Prosperous Life, new edition) by Masaharu Taniguchi.

7

積極的な明るい生き方から
「無限の可能性」が開かれる

　人生は心やコトバで作られる。だから明るいコトバと明るい心で、たのしくて嬉(うれ)しい毎日を送り、自分に埋(うも)れている「無限の可能性」を開発して行くことが大切である。すべてがもうすでに、あなたの中にアルのだ。ナイものは出せないが、アルものは、練習さえすれば、どんどん出て来るのである。

　　　　（谷口清超著『すばらしい未来を築こう』より）

Infinite possibilities grow from a positive and cheerful way of life.

Human life is created by mind and word. That is why it is important to spend your days happily and joyfully with cheerful words and a happy mind and develop the *infinite possibilities* that are buried within you. Everything is already within you. While what does not exist will not appear, what qualities exist will appear one after another if you only practice.

From *Subarashii Mirai o Kizukô* (Let Us Build a Wonderful Future) by Seicho Taniguchi.

8

「神の心」に波長が合うとき、豊かな人生が出現する

　吾々（われわれ）は「神の心」に波長を合わす心を起すことを第一にしなければならないのである。「神の心」に波長が合うとき、「神」は無限供給の源であるから、自然に物質的にも豊かな富が与えられて来るのである。内部の心の持方（もちかた）が大切であって、それさえ整えば自然に無限の富がやって来るのである。

（谷口雅春著『新版　希望を叶える365章』より）

When you are in tune with the *Mind of God*, an abundant life appears.

We must place the utmost importance on developing a mind that is in tune with the *Mind of God*. When we are in tune with the *Mind of God*, since *God* is the source of infinite supply, we are naturally given abundant wealth, including material wealth. Our mental attitude is important. If we only prepare our mind, infinite wealth will naturally come to us.

From *Shinpan Kibô o Kanaeru 365 Shô* (365 Keys to Realize Your Hopes, new edition) by Masaharu Taniguchi.

9

周囲の人々は、みな あなたの鏡である

　世界は自分の周囲に立て廻した鏡のようなものです。自分の「心」を映して見てそれを外界だと思うのです。少しく内省して見ると、自分の周囲には自分の「心」の結果ばかりがあらわれていることが分ります。「周囲を善くしようと思うならば先ず脚下照顧せよ」と云うのはそのゆえです。

（谷口雅春著『新版　真理』第2巻より）

The people around you are your mirror.

The world is like a mirror that revolves around us. We think of the reflection that is cast by our *mind* as being the outside world. With a little self-reflection we know that it is only the results of our *mind* that are manifested in our surroundings. That is why it is said: First reflect on yourself if you seek to improve your surroundings."

From *Shinpan Shinri* (Truth, new edition), vol. 2 by Masaharu Taniguchi.

10

病気を治すものは、自己の中の生命力である

　近頃は医学が発達したから、何でも医学に頼ればよいという人もおられるかも知れませんが、病気が治るのは本当は自然の癒(いや)す働きによるものです。これを「自然治癒力」といいます。この力は、人々に感謝し、世の中に感謝し、御祖先様に感謝しているような明るい心でいる時、一番よく現われて来るものです。

　　　　　　　　（谷口清超著『病いが消える』より）

The healer of illness is the life power within you.

There are people who think that medicine can be relied on for anything because of its recent advances. Nevertheless, what really heals illness is nature's healing work. We call this *natural healing power.* This power is strongest when you acquire a bright and cheerful mind that is grateful to people, the world and your ancestors.

From *Yamai ga Kieru* (Illness Vanishes) by Seicho Taniguchi.

11

「今」を真剣に生きるとき、一切の悩みや不幸は消える

　アセルことによって、問題は解決の方向に向わない。「無構え(むかま)」の心で、そのまま、ひたすら神をたたえ、神の子としての「今」を生きぬくことが大切である。「今」を真剣に生き切るとき、自意識過剰(かじょう)がなくなり、人を相手とせず天意を行(ぎょう)ずる者となるのである。そのとき忽然(こつねん)として、悩みや不幸はきえる。

　　　　　　　　（谷口清超著『人は天窓から入る』より）

When you sincerely live the *present moment*, all sufferings and misfortunes vanish.

Our problems do not improve by being impatient. It is important that we earnestly praise God, as He is, with a *genuine* heart and fully live the *present moment* as a child of God. When we sincerely live the *present moment* to the fullest, our oversensitiveness vanishes and we are no longer worried about what others may think but follow God's will. At that moment our sufferings and misfortunes suddenly vanish.

From *Hito wa Tenmado Kara Hairu* (We Enter From Heaven's Window) by Seicho Taniguchi.

12
人を赦(ゆる)し切ったとき、幸福の扉が開かれる

　「赦(ゆる)す」ということは、罪を大目に見ることではなく、相手の「神性(しんせい)」をみとめて、「罪なきもの」を再確認することである。この世の中には「認めるものが存在に入る」という原則がある。それ故、清浄(しょうじょう)なる心の者をみとめ、それを信ずる時、必ず神性・仏性(ぶっしょう)があらわれてくるという結果になるのである。

　　　　　　　（谷口清超新書文集４『真実を求めて』より）

When you forgive another completely, the door of happiness will open.

To forgive is not to overlook another's sin but to see the person's *Divinity* and reaffirm his *sinlessness*. In this world there is the fundamental rule that *what is recognized comes into existence.* That is why a person's Divinity and immanent Buddhahood surely appear when we recognize him as being pure-minded and believe in him.

From *Shinjitsu o Motomete* (Seeking Truth), Taniguchi Seicho Shinshobunshû, vol. 4.

13
父母（ちちはは）に感謝しえない者の人生は "切り花" の如（ごと）くである

　根があって枝葉（えだは）があるのです。親があって、子があるのです。親は根で、子孫は枝葉ですから、栄えようと思うものは親を大切にせねばなりません。親を大切に思う心は根を培（つちか）い、ひいては自分の生命（いのち）を延ばす本（もと）になるのです。どんな子が親を思うよりも以上に、親は子を愛しているのです。

（谷口雅春著『人生読本』より）

The lives of those who cannot be grateful to their parents are like "cut flowers."

It is because there are roots that there are branches and leaves. It is because of parents that there are children. Since parents are the roots and their descendants are the branches and leaves, those who want to prosper must take good care of their parents. The mind that treasures one's parents cultivates the roots and, in turn, it becomes the source for our life to grow. Parental love far exceeds any child's feelings for his parents.

From *Jinsei Dokuhon* (Life's Reader) by Masaharu Taniguchi.

14

自分自身に賞(ほ)められる人となれ

　他に見て貰って賞められたいと思うかわりに、自分の心で見て、自分自身を賞められるようにおなりなさい。自分の心に神の心が宿っているのですから、自分の心に賞められるのは神様に賞められるのも同じことです。だから自分で自分が賞められるようになったら、世の中でこんな楽しい事はありません。

　　　　　　　　　　　（谷口雅春著『人生読本』より）

Become a person who can praise himself.

Instead of seeking the attention and praise of others, see with your heart and become a person who can praise himself. Since the mind of God dwells within you, to praise yourself in your heart is the same as being praised by God. That is why there is nothing more delightful in this world than to be able to praise yourself.

From *Jinsei Dokuhon* (Life's Reader) by Masaharu Taniguchi.

15
他(た)の人の成功を悦(よろこ)べ、あなたは必ず成功する

　人の喜びを、共に喜ぶ心を喜心(きしん)という。人が成功したのを、あなたは心から共に喜べるだろうか。もしそれが出来なければ、それが出来るようになるまで、あなたの心を拡(ひろ)げるがよい。この作業によって、あなたは必ずより幸福になる。無限に豊かで美しく清(きよ)らかな世界を知ることができる。

（谷口清超著『伸びゆく日々の言葉』より）

Be happy for the success of others and you are sure to succeed.

The mind that rejoices in the joy of others is called the "joyful mind." Can you feel joy from the bottom of your heart for the success of another? If you cannot, you should expand your outlook on life until you can do so. Your efforts to expand your outlook will surely make you happier. You will come to know an infinitely abundant, beautiful and pure world.

From *Nobiyuku Hibi no Kotoba* (Daily Words for Growth) by Seicho Taniguchi.

16

去り行くものに感謝せよ、新しき良きものが来る

　去る者に執着(しゅうじゃく)して追ってはならない。去り行く者はあなたの魂に何物かを与える役目を果し終ったから去るのである。去る者に対して自分を裏切ったなどと憤(いか)りや恨(うら)みをもってはならない。去る者を感謝して放(はな)ち去ったとき、新しい友または伴侶(はんりょ)が来るための空席がしつらえられるのである。

　　　　　　（谷口雅春著『新版　女性の幸福 365 章』より）

Be grateful for what leaves you. Something new and better is on its way.

You must not hold fast to those who leave you or run after them. Those who leave are doing so because they have completed their role of helping your soul to grow. You must not be angry or hate a person for betraying your trust or the like. When you release him or her with gratitude in your heart, a seat for your new friend or companion will be prepared.

From *Shinpan Josei no Kôfuku 365 Shô* (365 Keys to Women's Happiness, new edition) by Masaharu Taniguchi.

17
人生勝利への道は、自分が主人公になることである

　人間は神さまから、"全ての力"を与えられている「神の子」だ。つまり「主人公」なのである。決して、運命や病気や災難に打ちまかされる弱虫ではない。そのことをはっきりと信じ、明るい深切(しんせつ)な心で生活すれば、必ず、その思う通りの幸福な人生を作り出すことができるのである。

　　　　　　　（谷口清超著『創造的人生のために』より）

The way to victory in life is for you to be its master.

Human beings are *children of God* who have been provided with "all power" from God. That is to say, they are the *master*. By no means are they weaklings that are defeated by destiny, illness or calamity. If we clearly believe this and live with happiness and kindness in our hearts, we will certainly create the happy life that we envision.

From *Sôzôteki Jinsei no Tame ni* (For a Creative Life) by Seicho Taniguchi.

18
夫婦は合せ鏡のように、互いの心を映し合う

　夫婦はちょうど合せ鏡のようなものです。こちらが憎々しげな姿をして鏡を見ると鏡の中の相手も憎々しげな顔をしてこちらをにらみ返しているでしょう。相手が変な顔の奴だと思っていても、実は本当は自分の姿が相手に映っている。そのように、夫婦はお互いに相手の心を映し出しているのです。
　（谷口清超ヒューマン・ブックス5『女性教室』より）

Husband and wife are like mirrors placed opposite each other. They reflect each other's thoughts.

Husband and wife are like mirrors placed opposite each other. When we look into the mirror with a hateful look, the reflection in the mirror will also glare at us in the same way. While we may complain about the strange look on a person's face, the fact is that our own image is reflected by his person. In this way husband and wife reflect their thoughts on one another.

From *Josei Kyôshitsu* (Classroom for Women), Taniguchi Seicho Human Books, vol. 5.

19
自己に打克つ者こそ最大の強者である

　自己の心を支配する者のみ、自分の運命を支配することが出来る。人間の心は誠に複雑なものであって、自分の心の中に自己を不幸や貧乏に突き落す「自己破壊」の獅子身中の虫のような心があるのである。自己に克つ者は最大の強者であると言うのは自己破壊の「ニセモノ」の自分に打ち克つからである。

　　　　　　　　（谷口雅春著『新版　真理』第2巻より）

He who overcomes himself is indeed the strongest of all.

Only those who rule their mind can control their destiny. The human mind is truly complex. Within our mind there is a treacherous friend of *self-destruction* that thrust us into misfortune or poverty. He who overcomes himself is the strongest of all because he defeats his *false self* of self-destruction.

From *Shinpan Shinri* (Truth, new edition), vol. 2 by Masaharu Taniguchi.

20

積極的な祈りとは、すばらしい実相を観る「神想観」である

「神想観」は、単なる祈りではありません。神の国・実相世界・本当にある世界を、じっと心の眼で観るのです。あらゆるよいものが満ちあふれている、神の国そのものを、じっと心の眼で観るのです。すると、自然と神の国のすばらしい才能や豊かさや楽しいことが続々と出てくるようになるものです。

（谷口清超著『神想観はすばらしい』より）

A positive prayer is *Shinsokan* that sees the wonderful True Image.

Shinsokan is not simply a prayer. It is to steadily see with our mind's eye the Kingdom of God, the True-Image World and the Real World. We steadily see with our mind's eye the Kingdom of God Itself that is brimming over with every good thing. The result is that the wonderful abilities, abundance and happiness of the Kingdom of God appear in our lives naturally one after another.

From *Shinsokan wa Subarashii* (Shinsokan Is Wonderful) by Seicho Taniguchi.

21
一切万事を自己の責任と自覚せよ、あなたは日々生長する

　一切万事我(われ)より出でて我(かえ)に還るのである。自分の不幸も幸福も、一切万事、自分の心の持方(もちかた)によって展開してくるということを悟(さと)りますと、何事が起こって来ましょうとも、責任を自分に帰して、他(ひと)を怨(うら)まず、憎(にく)まず、自己を反省し、自己改革に専念するようになれるのであります。

　　　　（谷口雅春著『生命の根元を培う新しき教育』より）

Realize that you are responsible for all things!
You will grow by the day.

All things come forth from me and return to me. My misfortune and happiness and all things develop according to the direction of my mind. When I awaken to this truth, no matter what may happen, it is my responsibility and I do not think ill of or hate another but reflect on myself and concentrate on my self-improvement.

From *Seimei no Kongen o Tsuchikau Atarashiki Kyôiku* (New Education That Cultivates the Source of Life) by Masaharu Taniguchi.

22
父母に感謝せぬ者は神の御心にかなわぬ

　我々にとって、父母は「神」の代行者でもあるのです。父母への反抗は「神」に反逆するところの行為でありますから、幸福を自らの手で奪い取ってしまうのです。ところがこれと反対に、自分自身が"神の子"であることを知り、父母を愛し敬する者は、祝福された人生を送るのであります。

（谷口清超ヒューマン・ブックス2『運命の主人公』より）

Those who are not grateful to their parents go against the Divine Will.

Our parents are indeed *God's* agent for us. To disobey them is treason against *God*, and that is why happiness will be stolen from us through our own hands. On the other hand, those who know that they are "children of God" and love and respect their parents, will live a life of blessings.

From *Unmei no Shujinkô* (Master of Destiny), Taniguchi Seicho Human Books, vol. 2.

23

最後まで望みを捨てず
努力する者は必ず報われる

　希望は現実ではない。それは未来への夢だ。しかし、その夢は実現しうるのである。何故なら、実相において既に実現しているからだ。たとい一時挫折するように見えても、人生を放棄しない限り、必ず実現する。それ故、現象にふりまわされ、失望落胆するな。あなたは、無限に生き続ける神の子である。

　　　　　（谷口清超著『伸びゆく日々の言葉』より）

Those who do not give up hope, but make an effort to the very end, are sure to be rewarded.

Your hopes are not the actualities. They are dreams for the future. Those dreams, however, can be realized. That is because they are already realized in the True Image. Even when it seems that you have failed, your dreams will surely be realized as long as you do not give up. That is why you must not be confused by phenomena and lose hope and courage. You are children of God who continue to live infinitely.

From *Nobiyuku Hibi no Kotoba* (Daily Words for Growth) by Seicho Taniguchi.

24
「天才」はすべての人の中に すでにある

　全(すべ)ての人々の中に「天才」がある。神(天)はごく一部の者にしか才(さい)を与え給わないというエコヒイキはなさらない。だから全ての人々に「天才」がある。人は内在の力を現(あら)わし出してこそ楽しく嬉(うれ)しいのである。それ故(ゆえ)全ての人々は、すでに与えられている「天才」をみとめ、それを現わし出す練習をしよう。

（谷口清超著『伸びゆく日々の言葉』より）

A *genius* already dwells within everyone.

Everyone has a *genius* within himself. Heaven is not partial in giving talents to one single group. That is why there is a *genius* in everyone. When people manifest their inner power they feel happiness and joy. Therefore, let everyone recognize the *genius* that he has been given and train himself to manifest it.

From *Nobiyuku Hibi no Kotoba* (Daily Words for Growth) by Seicho Taniguchi.

25

心の眼(め)をひらけ、幸福はいたるところに手を広げて待っている

　人生には美しいもの、貴(とうと)いもの、感動的行為など、いくらでもころがっている。生き甲斐ある生活を送ろうと思うならば、即刻(そっこく)「宝さがし」を始めよう。探す気になればいくらでも「美しさ」が見出(みいだ)される。人の美点、美しい自然、貴い思いやりなど、小さな宝石のように、いくらでもちりばめられている。

　　　　　　　　（谷口清超著『輝く日々のために』より）

Open your mind's eye and everywhere happiness awaits you with open arms.

In human life there are any amount of beautiful and precious things and inspirational deeds and the like. If you seek to live a life that is worth living, immediately begin your *treasure hunt*. Any amount of *beauty* can be discovered if you want to find it. Like precious gems, any amount of good points, beautiful natural surroundings and precious, kind deeds, and the like, are everywhere present.

From *Kagayaku Hibi no Tame ni* (For a Shining Daily Life) by Seicho Taniguchi.

26

あなたは神から祝福された神の子である

　毎朝の生活の出発の時"神の子"なる汝の実相を念じて、その実相の足基の上に立ち、実相の燈火に照らされて歩むがよい。神の智慧は汝を導き、神の愛は汝を護る。神の愛は如何なる敵意よりも強く、神の智慧は如何なる悪しき奸計よりも慧いのである。汝は神の子、神から祝福されたるものである。

（谷口雅春著『人生の祕訣365章』より）

You are a child of God blessed by God.

Every morning, at the start of the day, meditate on your True Image that is a "child of God," stand upon the foundation of the True Image and walk with the light of the True Image. God's wisdom guides you and His love protects you. God's love is stronger than any evil intentions and His wisdom is keener than all evil designs. You are a child of God who is blessed by God.

From *Jinsei no Hiketsu 365 Shô* (365 Keys to the Secret of Human Life) by Masaharu Tanigchi.

27
優しい言葉が自然に湧いてくるような人は、全ての人から愛される

　あなたは太陽のように、温かさと明るさを周囲になげかけなければなりません。明るいところへは人がよろこんで集まってくるのです。あなたは冬になると日向ぼっこをしたいでしょう。温かいところを人は愛して集まって来るのです。人を愛すれば、人から愛されます。人を喜ばせば、人から喜ばれます。

（谷口雅春著『新版　真理』第3巻より）

A person who speaks kind words with naturalness and ease will be loved by all.

You must spread warmth and happiness to those around you like the shining sun. People happily gather at a place that is bright and cheerful. Don't you like to sit in the sun during the winter? People love warmth and gather where there is warmth. People will be loved if they love others. They will be made happy if they make others happy.

From *Shinpan Shinri* (Truth, new edition), vol. 3 by Masaharu Taniguchi.

28

「愛」は惜(お)しまず表現することによって実を結ぶ

　愛や知恵は誰にでもある。しかし単にあるだけでは「悦(よろこ)び」の体験とはならないのである。アルものを現わし出して、始めて悦びとして体験される。あなたは妻に対し、夫に対し、愛のコトバをどれだけ話しかけたか。愛の表情をどれだけ表わしたか。愛は才能と同じく、蔽(おお)われたままでは悦べないのである。

（谷口清超著『伸びゆく日々の言葉』より）

Love bears fruit by giving of itself unstintingly.

All people have love and wisdom. However, simple possession of these virtues does not become an experience of *joy*. We experience joy for the first time when we manifest what we possess. How many loving words have you spoken to your wife or husband? How often have you kept a loving expression on your face? Love is like an ability. There is no happiness when love remains hidden.

From *Nobiyuku Hibi no Kotoba* (Daily Words for Growth) by Seicho Taniguchi.

29
悦びを語るとき、悦びは限りなく増幅する

　よろこび、よろこぶところに喜びが集まってくる。昨日もよろこび、今日もよろこび、明日もよろこぶ。よろこぶ心で世界を見ればみんながよろこんでいる。空気がよろこび、新緑がよろこび、小鳥がよろこび、人間がよろこんでいる。わたしの仕事はただよろこぶことだけである。

（谷口雅春著『生命の實相』頭注版第37巻より）

Speak of joy, and joy increases boundlessly.

Where there is joy and where people rejoice is where happiness gathers. Yesterday was delightful. Today is the same and so is tomorrow. Everything seems happy when we see the world with a joyful mind. The air is rejoicing and so are the fresh leaves, the little birds and human beings. My work is to simply rejoice.

From *Seimei no Jissô* (Truth of Life), vol. 37 by Masaharu Taniguchi.

30
「創造的な祈り」は、人の魂を高貴ならしめる

　人間は皆神の子ですから、誰でも生まれたときは、神の御心そのままのきれいな心をもっています。もしあなたが人から信用され、愛され、あなたの天性を発揮するすばらしい人になりたいのなら、もう一度神の御心と直結したらよいのです。神の御心と直結するための最も良い方法が「神想観」なのです。

　　　　　（谷口清超著『神想観はすばらしい』より）

A *creative prayer* will elevate your soul.

Since human beings are all children of God, from birth everyone is the possessor of a mind that is as pure as the original condition of the Mind of God. If you seek to become a person who is trusted and loved by others, and a wonderful person who demonstrates his real nature, you should once again link yourself directly with the mind of God. The best method to be directly linked with God is *Shinsokan.*

From *Shinsokan wa Subarashii* (Shinsokan Is Wonderful) by Seicho Taniguchi.

31

愛の前には敵がない、すべてのものが味方となる

　善の前には悪はおのずから消えてしまうのである。われは神と偕(とも)であるが故に、すべての恐怖と、怒りと、劣等感は拭(ぬぐ)いさられたのである。われはなにものをも恐れない。私はすべての人を愛する。それ故(ゆえ)に、彼をも愛するのである。愛は無敵である。愛の前には敵はない。すべてのものは味方となるのである。

　　　　　　　（谷口雅春著『私はこうして祈る』より）

In the face of love there is no adversary. Everyone becomes a friend.

In the presence of goodness, evil vanishes of its own accord. Since I am one with God, all fear, anger and sense of inferiority have been wiped away. I fear nothing. I love all people. That is why they also love me. Love is invincible. There are no enemies in the presence of love. Everyone becomes a friend.

From *Watashi wa Kôshite Inoru* (This Is How I Pray) by Masaharu Taniguchi.

参考図書

谷口雅春著　聖経版　真理の吟唱
谷口清超ヒューマン・ブックス2　運命の主人公
谷口雅春著　人生読本
谷口清超　輝く日々のために
谷口雅春著　新版　栄える生活365章
谷口清超ヒューマン・ブックス6　人生の開拓者
谷口清超　智慧と愛のメッセージ
新選谷口雅春法話集5　光明道中記
谷口清超　純粋に生きよう
谷口雅春著　新版　真理　第9巻
谷口雅春著　新版　真理　第1巻
谷口清超ヒューマン・ブックス9　善意の世界
谷口清超新書文集5　「愛」は勝利する
谷口雅春著作集第9巻　幸福の哲学
谷口清超著　伸びゆく日々の言葉
谷口雅春著 新版　光明法語〈道の巻〉
谷口清超著　妻として母として
谷口清超著　如意自在の生活365章
谷口清超ヒューマン・ブックス1　愛と祈りを実現するには
谷口雅春著　生命の實相　頭注版第38巻
谷口清超新書文集6　サラリーマンの精神衛生
谷口雅春著　新版　叡智の断片
谷口雅春著　生命の實相　頭注版第20巻
谷口清超新書文集3　もっと幸福になれる
谷口雅春著　聖経版　続　真理の吟唱
谷口清超著　自己完成のために
谷口雅春著　新版　女性の幸福365章
谷口清超著　私はこうして祈る
谷口清超著　人は天窓から入る
谷口清超ヒューマン・ブックス4　生きる
谷口清超著　ステキな生き方がある
谷口雅春著　新版　生活の智慧365章
谷口清超著　病いが消える
谷口雅春著　生命の實相　頭注版第7巻
谷口雅春著　親と子の愛について
谷口雅春著　青年の書
谷口雅春著　新版　幸福を招く365章
谷口雅春著　新版　真理　第2巻
谷口清超著　創造的人生のために
谷口雅春著　生命の實相　頭注版第22巻
谷口清超著　すばらしい未来を築こう
谷口雅春著　新版　希望を叶える365章
谷口清超新書文集4　真実を求めて
谷口清超ヒューマン・ブックス5　女性教室
谷口清超著　神想観はすばらしい
谷口雅春著　生命の根元を培う新しき教育
谷口雅春著　人生の祕訣365章
谷口雅春著　新版　真理　第3巻
谷口雅春著　生命の實相　頭注版第37巻

上記図書はすべて日本教文社刊

References

Masaharu Taniguchi. *Seikyôban Shinri no Ginshô* (Meditations on Truth, sutra edition).

Seicho Taniguchi. *Unmei no Shujinkô* (Master of Destiny), Taniguchi Seicho Human Books, vol. 2.

Masaharu Taniguchi. *Jinsei Dokuhon* (Life's Reader).

Seicho Taniguchi. *Kagayaku Hibi no Tame ni* (For a Shining Daily Life).

Masaharu Taniguchi. *Shinpan Sakaeru Seikatsu 365 Shô* (365 Keys to a Prosperous Life, new edition).

Seicho Taniguchi. *Jinsei no Kaitakusha* (Pioneers of Human Life), Taniguchi Seicho Human Books, vol. 6.

———. *Chie to Ai no Message* (Messages of Wisdom and Love).

Masaharu Taniguchi. *Komyô Dôchûki* (Record of the Journey of Light), Shinsen Taniguchi Masaharu Hôwashû, vol. 5.

Seicho Taniguchi. *Junsui ni Ikyô* (Let Us Live a Pure Life).

Masaharu Taniguchi. *Shinpan Shinri* (Truth, new edition), vol. 9.

———. *Shinpan Shinri* (Truth, new edition), vol. 1.

Seicho Taniguchi. *Zen-i no Sekai* (World of Good Intentions), Taniguchi Seicho Human Books, vol. 9.

———. *"Ai" wa Shôrisuru* (Love Wins), Taniguchi Seicho Shinsho Bunshu, vol. 5.

Masaharu Taniguchi. *Kôfuku no Tetsugaku* (Philosophy of Happiness), Taniguchi Masaharu Chosakushû, vol. 9.

Seicho Taniguchi. *Nobiyuku Hibi no Kotoba* (Daily Words for Growth).

Masaharu Taniguchi. *Shinpan Kômyôhôgo: Michi no Maki* (Sermons on Light: Volume on the Way, new edition).

Seicho Taniguchi. *Tsuma Toshite Haha Toshite* (As a Wife and Mother).

Masaharu Taniguchi. *Nyoi Jizai no Seikatsu 365 Shô* (365 Golden Keys to a Completely Free Life).

Seicho Taniguchi. *Ai to Inori o Jitsugensuru ni wa* (To Realize Love and Prayer), Taniguchi Seicho Human Books, vol. 1.

Masaharu Taniguchi. *Seimei no Jissô* (Truth of Life), vol. 38.

Seicho Taniguchi. *Sarari-man no Seishin Eisei* (A Salaried Man's Mental Hygiene), Taniguchi Seicho Shinshobunshû, vol. 6.

Masaharu Taniguchi. *Shinpan Eichi no Danpen* (Short Pieces of Wisdom, new edition).

———. *Seimei no Jissô* (Truth of Life), vol. 20.

Seicho Taniguchi. *Motto Kôfuku ni Nareru* (We Can Become Happier), Taniguchi Seicho Shinshobunshû, vol. 3.

Masaharu Taniguchi. *Seikyôban Zoku Shinri no Ginshô* (Meditations on Truth II, sutra edition).

Masaharu Taniguchi. *Jiko Kansei no Tame ni* (For Our Self-Perfection).

Masaharu Taniguchi. *Shinpan Josei no Kôfuku 365 Sho* (365 Keys to Women's Happiness, new edition).

———. *Watashi wa Kôshite Inoru* (This Is How I Pray).

Seicho Taniguchi. *Hito wa Tenmado Kara Hairu* (We Enter From Heaven's Window).

———. *Ikiru* (To Live) Taniguchi Seicho Human Books, vol. 4.

———. *Sutekina Ikikata ga Aru* (There Is a Fine Way to Live).

Masaharu Taniguchi. *Shinpan Seikatsu no Chie 365 Sho* (365 Keys to Daily Wisdom, new edition).

Seicho Taniguchi. *Yamai ga Kieru* (Illness Vanishes).

Masaharu Taniguchi. *Seimei no Jissô* (Truth of Life), vol. 7.

Seicho Taniguchi. *Oya to Ko no Ai ni Tsuite* (About the Love of Parent and Child).

Masaharu Taniguchi. *Seinen no Sho* (For Young People).

———. *Shinpan Kôfuku o Maneku 355 Shô* (365 Keys That Summon Happiness, new edition).

———. *Shinpan Shinri* (Truth, new edition), vol. 2.

Seicho Taniguchi. *Sôzôteki Jinsei no Tame ni* (For a Creative Life).

Masaharu Taniguchi. *Seimei no Jissô* (Truth of Life), vol. 22.

Seicho Taniguchi. *Subarashii Mirai o Kizukô* (Let Us Build a Wonderful Future).

Masaharu Taniguchi. *Shinpan Kibô o Kanaeru 365 Shô* (365 Keys to Realize Your Hopes, new edition).

Seicho Taniguchi. *Shinjitsu o Motomete* (Seeking Truth), Taniguchi Seicho Shinshobunshû, vol. 4.

———. *Josei Kyôshitsu* (Classroom for Women), Taniguchi Seicho Human Books, vol. 5.

———. *Shinsokan wa Subarashii* (Shinsokan Is Wonderful).

Masaharu Taniguchi. *Seimei no Kongea o Tsuchikau Atarashiki Kyôiku* (New Education That Cultivates the Source of Life).

———. *Jinsei no Hiketsu 365 Shô* (365 Keys to the Secret of Human Life).

———. *Shinpan Shinri* (Truth, new edition), vol. 3.

———. *Seimei no Jissô* (Truth of Life), vol. 37.

Above books are published by Nippon Kyobunsha Co. Ltd.

人生の扉を開く《第4集》― 日英対訳で読む　ひかりの言葉 ―

2008年11月15日　初版第1刷発行
2022年10月 1 日　初版第2刷発行

監修者………谷口清超　〈検印省略〉© Seicho-No-Ie, 2008
英訳…………牧之段高男ディーン
監訳…………クリストファー・ノートンウェルシュ
発行者………西尾慎也
発行所………株式会社 日本教文社
　　　　　　　東京都港区赤坂 9-6-44 〒107-8674
　　　　　　　電話　03（3401）9111（代表）
　　　　　　　　　　03（3401）9114（編集）
　　　　　　　FAX　03（3401）9118（編集）
　　　　　　　　　　03（3401）9139（営業）
　　　　　　　https://www.kyobunsha.co.jp/
頒布所………一般財団法人 世界聖典普及協会
　　　　　　　東京都港区赤坂 9-6-33 〒107-8691
　　　　　　　電話　03（3403）1501（代表）
　　　　　　　振替　00110-7-120549
印刷…………港北メディアサービス株式会社
製本…………牧製本印刷株式会社
カバー挿画……鯰江光二
デザイン………株式会社アクロバット　佐藤憲／江本祐介

◆……………乱丁本・落丁本はお取り替えいたします。
◆……………定価はカバーに表示してあります。

本書（本文）の紙は植林木を原料としています。また、印刷インクに大豆インク（ソイインク）を使用することで、環境に配慮した本造りを行っています。

ISBN978-4-531-05262-2　Printed in Japan